FOCUS ON DISASTERS

Weather

Fred Martin

RIGBY
INTERACTIVE
LIBRARY

Designed by Raynor Design

Produced by Mandarin Offset Ltd.
Printed and bound in Hong Kong

99 98 97 96 95
10 9 8 7 6 5 4 3 2 1

ISBN 1-57572-022-1

Library of Congress Cataloguing in Publication Data

Martin, Fred. 1948–
    Weather/Fred Martin.
         p. cm.–(Focus on Disasters)
    Includes index.
    Summary: Examines how and why destructive
    weather happens, its effects upon people and
    the environment, and what is being done to
    prevent future devastation.
    ISBN 1-57572-022-1 (lib.bdg.)
    1. Weather–Juvenile literature.
    2. Meteorology–Juvenile literature.
    3. Storms–Juvenile literature. [1. Weather.
    2. Meteorology. 3. Storms.] I. Title.
    II. Series. Martin. Fred. 1948– Focus on
    Disasters.
    QC981.3.M367 1996
    363.3'492–dc20   95-38353

Acknowledgments
The Publishers would like to thank the following for permission to reproduce
photographs:
Ace Photo Agency: p. 39; Brown/SABA/REA/Katz Pictures Ltd: p. 41; Bruce
Coleman Ltd: p. 19; Bruce Coleman Ltd/Francisco Futil: p. 34; Karly Carlson: p. 22;
Colorific: p. 29; Frank Lane Picture Agency: p. 42; Frank Spooner Pictures: pp. 25, 30,
31, 40; GeoScience Features: p. 10; Ben Gibson/Katz Pictures Ltd: p. 45; J. Allan Cash
Photo Library: pp. 4, 9, 14, 15, 38; Kees/Sygma: p. 26; Panos Pictures/Jeremy
Hartley: pp. 35, 37; Panos Pictures/Penny Tweedie: p. 36; Rex Features: p. 17; Robert
Harding Picture Library: p. 32; Science Photo Library/Howard Bluestein: p. 28;
Science Photo Library/European Space Agency: p. 13; Science Photo Library/Keith
Kent: p. 18; Science Photo Library/Peter Menzel: p. 16; Science Photo Library/NASA:
pp. 6, 21, 33; Science Photo Library/NASA Goddard Institute for Space Studies: p. 44;
Science Photo Library/David Pancer: p. 8; Steve Stan/SABA/Katz Pictures Ltd: p. 24;
Still Pictures/Mark Edwards: pp. 5, 43; Topham Picturepoint: p. 27; Zefa UK
Limited: p. 9.

Cover photograph © Tony Stone Worldwide

Contents

People and the Weather

EVERYBODY has an interest in the weather. The weather affects almost everything we do. We depend on it for the basics that we need to survive.

Water to drink comes from rain. The food we eat needs sun and rain to grow. What we do outside is affected by the weather, and our homes have to be designed to keep us warm and dry.

Weather Extremes

It takes a human disaster to remind us what the weather can do. Disasters usually occur when the weather is unusual. It is not always easy to predict these extremes of weather. Weather extremes are different in different parts of the world. Rainfall of 14 inches in one month is common in those parts of Asia with a **monsoon climate**. In most parts of the United States, a month with half that rainfall would be almost unknown.

Average winter **temperatures** in the United States at or near freezing point would be extreme for Africa or northern Australia.

People adapt their way of life to the weather that is normal for where they live. Farmers grow crops that are suited to the temperature and rainfall in their area. Houses are built in different shapes and with different materials to suit local conditions. In some places, steep roofs help **snow** to slide off more easily. A flat roof is useful if the weather is hotter and people want to sleep on it. The problems come when we suddenly have to cope with weather that is not suited to our way of life.

Photo Notes

- Weather that people should expect on a vacation.
- Campers and tents give enough protection from rain, cold, and heat, but are sometimes not strong enough to survive strong winds.
- An umbrella is always useful as the summer can be predicted to be unpredictable!

Lessons from the Braer

In January 1993, the Braer oil tanker ran aground on the coast of the Shetland Islands. Its engine had stopped as it was passing by the islands about 9 miles to the south. Seawater got into the fuel as waves 93 feet high broke over the ship.

By 6:00 A.M., the tanker was unable to steer. **Gale** force **winds** continued to blow from the south. By 9:30 A.M., the crew had been taken off the tanker by helicopter. The coast was getting closer every minute. A tug tried to tow the Braer away, but the sea was too rough. At 11:30 A.M., the tanker hit the rocks and began to spill its oil. There was nothing more that anyone could have done to save it.

Waves battered the tanker for the next few days until it was a broken hulk. The gale made it impossible to bring another tanker alongside to take off the rest of the oil. Booms could not be used to stop the oil from spreading. Fortunately, the fierce winds also did some good. They helped the sea to break up the oil so that it did not form an oil slick that would have washed up on the nearby shores.

Photo Notes

- The Braer tanker ran aground on the Shetland Islands in January 1993.
- Gale force winds caused the ship's engine to stop then blew the tanker onto the rocks.
- The weather affected rescue plans in a way that had not been predicted.

The Braer's captain had been following a route that was thought to be safe. There were emergency plans in case an oil tanker did have problems in the area. But these plans did not take into account the fierce weather that caused the tanker to stop and then blow it on the rocks.

The weather that struck the Braer was extreme, though gales like this can be expected at least once a year in that area. It seems that plans for the future will need to be rewritten.

DID YOU KNOW? ?

The world's wettest place used to be in Hawaii. It is now at Mawsynram in northeast India. The average rainfall is 463 inches per year. The average rainfall on the earth each year is 34 inches.

The Weather Layer

A LAYER of gases about 620 miles deep surrounds the earth. This layer is called the **atmosphere**. There would be no life on earth without the gases in this layer. We need its oxygen to breathe and plants need its **carbon dioxide** to grow. The **water vapor** that evaporates from the sea becomes rain to give us water to drink.

Heat from the Sun

The atmosphere is divided into several different layers up to 500 miles above the earth. The highest layer is called the **thermosphere**. Beneath this is the **mesosphere**, stretching from 150 miles to 250 miles above the earth.

Below the mesosphere is the **stratosphere**. Weather balloons and some aircraft go up into this layer. At about 30 miles, a layer of **ozone** gas helps block out harmful ultraviolet rays from the sun. Gases in this layer are very thin, so heat from the sun is not absorbed. There is little water vapor, so there are no clouds.

The lowest layer is called the **troposphere**. This is where all our weather takes place. The weather is what happens to the temperature, winds, and rainfall day by day. Months when the same kind of weather can be expected are put into groups called **seasons**. The **climate** of an area describes what the average weather conditions are like throughout the year.

The sun's heat gives the energy that causes different weather. Heat beams down through the atmosphere until it reaches the earth's surface. Some of the heat is

Photo Notes
- The earth from space.
- Clouds form where there is water vapor in the lower layer of the atmosphere called the troposphere.
- Other gases in the upper layers of the atmosphere cannot be seen.

reflected back to space. Gases in the atmosphere absorb some of this reflected heat and keep it in the troposphere.

Unequal Heat

Some parts of the earth get more heat than others. More heat reaches the ground where the sun's rays travel at a high angle through the atmosphere. This is what happens near the equator, where the sun is sometimes directly overhead.

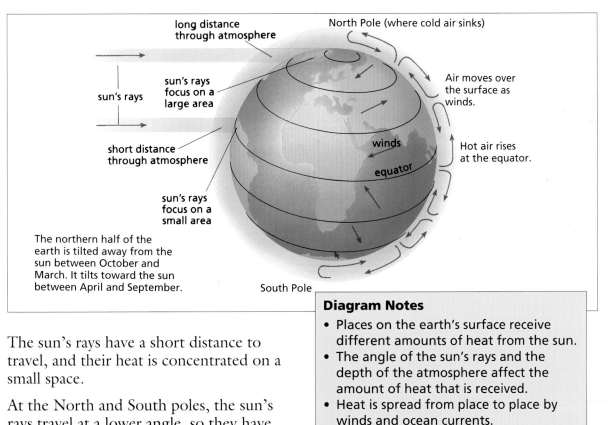

long distance through atmosphere

North Pole (where cold air sinks)

sun's rays

sun's rays focus on a large area

Air moves over the surface as winds.

short distance through atmosphere

winds

Hot air rises at the equator.

equator

sun's rays focus on a small area

The northern half of the earth is tilted away from the sun between October and March. It tilts toward the sun between April and September.

South Pole

The sun's rays have a short distance to travel, and their heat is concentrated on a small space.

At the North and South poles, the sun's rays travel at a lower angle, so they have further to go. When they reach the earth, their heat spreads out over a large area, so the ground is heated less. It is like shining a flashlight at a low angle rather than directly from above.

Light surfaces, such as snow and ice, reflect back more heat than dark surfaces, such as forests. This makes the polar areas even colder.

The earth spins around at an angle that points the North Pole and the South Pole toward the sun at different times of the year. This changes the angle of the sun's rays from season to season. The northern half of the earth, called the northern **hemisphere**, points toward the sun between April and September. It points away from the sun between October and March. This means that the amount of heat reaching the ground is different from season to season.

Heat that reaches the earth's surface does not stay in the same place. Warm air rises, then spreads out in the upper layers of the

Diagram Notes
- Places on the earth's surface receive different amounts of heat from the sun.
- The angle of the sun's rays and the depth of the atmosphere affect the amount of heat that is received.
- Heat is spread from place to place by winds and ocean currents.

troposphere. Cold air sinks then flows across the surface. This causes the winds.

There is a pattern to these winds that is called **global circulation**. This circulation helps reduce the extremes of hot and cold that would build up around the equator and the poles. Winds sometimes bring an unusual amount of heat or cold from one place to another. This helps to cause some weather extremes that can create such problems.

DID YOU KNOW? ?

Winds should blow in straight lines between places. Instead, they are deflected, because the earth is spinning. In the northern half of the earth, winds are deflected to the right, and in the southern half to the left. This turning effect is called the Corriolis force.

Weather Watching

It is easy to see and feel the difference between a hot summer's day and one in winter when there is snow on the ground. It is also easy to see when it is raining and roughly how much has fallen. On some days, the air may even feel damp though it may not be raining. Words such as "hot" and "wet" give a general description of the weather. Figures are needed to make descriptions more accurate.

Measuring the weather helps make predictions about what is to come.

A prediction made about the weather is called a **weather forecast**. Weather disasters can cause more damage when they are not accurately forecast.

Temperature

The amount of heat is given by a number for temperature. A **thermometer** is used to measure temperature. Temperature affects every part of the weather including the amount of rainfall, **pressure**, and winds.

Warm air is able to evaporate and hold more moisture than cold air. It does this by changing water into water vapor. When the temperature of moist air is reduced, the water vapor condenses back to tiny droplets of water and ice. This is how clouds, then rain and snow, are formed.

When air rises to go over a mountain, it expands and cools. Water vapor soon turns to clouds then rain. This is why mountain areas are usually wetter than lowland areas. On hot days in summer, air is warmed by the ground and starts to rise. This is called **convection**. The air rises in a current called a **thermal**. If the air keeps rising, **thunderstorms** can form, and the rainfall can be very heavy.

Photo Notes
- A weather station with instruments to record wind speed and direction, temperature, and the amount of moisture and sunshine.
- The recordings are entered on a portable computer.

Weather Details

The amount of rain is measured by seeing how much falls into a tube called a **rain gauge**. The word **precipitation** is used to include all types of moisture that falls to the ground. Rain, snow, sleet, and **hail** are all types of precipitation. A depth of 12 inches of snow is about the same as 1 inch of rain.

Studying clouds can give clues to what the weather is going to do. Large, billowing clouds are called **cumulus** clouds. They can bring a mixture of sunshine and showers. Some clouds are in thick layers. They are called **stratus** clouds. Low stratus clouds often bring continuous heavy rain and drizzle. **Cirrus** clouds are the highest level clouds. They are usually a sign of good weather, but if the clouds begin to get lower, watch out for rain and stronger winds to come.

Clouds affect the amount of sunshine. Vacation resorts like to give figures that show their **sunshine hours**.

Wind speed is measured using an **anemometer**. Small cups are spun around by the wind to give a speed reading. The wind direction is shown by seeing which way an arrow points on a **weather vane**.

Pressure is the weight of air that presses down on the ground. People cannot see or feel it, but it can be measured on a **barometer** or a **barograph**.

Some of the worst extremes of weather are caused by very high pressure or by very low pressure.

Figures that show the climate for an area are often given in a simple chart. There is usually a figure for temperature and rainfall for each month. These are average figures that do not show the maximum (highest) or the minimum (lowest) in the month. The figures have been taken from the averages over many years, so they do not show how different each year's weather can be. Weather extremes are hidden by these average figures. It is usually the extremes of weather that cause problems.

DID YOU KNOW? [?]

Glider pilots look for signs of convection. They use thermals to gain height in the same way that birds spiral upward in rising air.

Understanding Pressure

THE weight of air in the atmosphere presses down on us. We do not feel this pressure, because our bodies press back. The force of air is called **air pressure**. Information about air pressure is useful in making weather forecasts.

Pressure and Winds

Air pressure is affected by the temperature. Warm air rises and cold air sinks. If the air is rising, the pressure on the ground is lower. This gives an area of low pressure.

When air sinks, it presses down on the ground, giving an area of high pressure.

The amount of pressure is shown on a map by lines called **isobars**. These are like contour lines drawn on maps to show height. Pressure is measured in millibars.

Air moves from areas of high pressure to areas of low pressure. This causes winds.

Blow up a balloon, then release the air to see what happens. Air inside the balloon is at a higher pressure than the air outside. Once the air is released, it rushes out until the pressure inside and outside the balloon is the same again.

Winds blow faster when there is a large difference in air pressure over a short distance. This difference is called the **pressure gradient**. You can see this on a weather map when the isobars are close together. Pressure affects the amount of clouds and rain. Clouds and rain form when air is rising and cooling (low pressure). There is less chance of clouds and rain when air is sinking and being warmed (high pressure).

Photo Notes
- A barograph measures the weight of air pressing on the ground.
- The line has just traced a period of high pressure.
- Measurements for pressure are usually given in millibars.

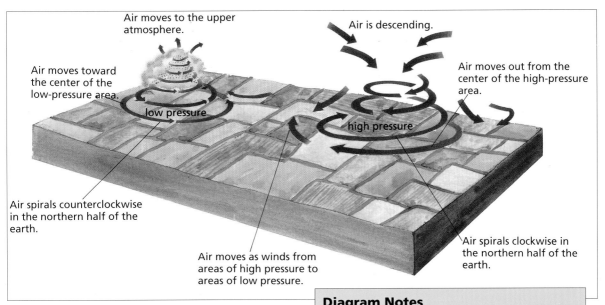

Air moves to the upper atmosphere.

Air moves toward the center of the low-pressure area.

low pressure

Air spirals counterclockwise in the northern half of the earth.

Air is descending.

Air moves out from the center of the high-pressure area.

high pressure

Air spirals clockwise in the northern half of the earth.

Air moves as winds from areas of high pressure to areas of low pressure.

Diagram Notes
- The weight of air pressing down is called air pressure.

Pressure Systems

An area of high pressure forms when the air sinks over a large area. This is called an **anticyclone**. Giant anticyclones form over continents during winter as cold air sinks toward the earth. They form over central Asia and North America during the winter months. There are also places where air that was heated and then rose at the equator starts to sink and forms high pressure areas.

When light winds blow out from an anticyclone, the weather is usually very settled. In winter, this can bring a long period of very cold weather. In summer, an anticyclone brings a long period of calm and very hot weather. There may be no rain for weeks. Some of the worst **drought** periods come when there is an anticyclone. The type of weather depends on the time of year and where the air comes from.

A **low-pressure system** is an area of low air pressure. The air spirals inward and upward. People often talk about a **cyclone** or a **hurricane** to mean an area where the pressure is very much lower than usual. These special areas of very low pressure are called **typhoons** in Southeast Asia and **willy-willies** in Australia.

Winds spiral around the high and low-pressure areas. They move faster toward the center of a low-pressure area and more slowly around the center of a high-pressure area. The air spirals out from an anticyclone in a clockwise direction in the northern half of the earth. It spins counterclockwise around areas of low pressure. The opposite happens in the southern hemisphere. Winds should blow in a straight line between the centers of high and low pressure, but they are deflected as the earth spins around.

Extreme areas of high and low pressure are the cause of most weather disasters. They cause the hottest and coldest months, the wettest and driest seasons, and the strongest winds. This is why **meteorologists** find it so important to measure air pressure.

DID YOU KNOW? **?**

Pressure decreases with height. This is why a pressure reading can be used to measure the height of an airplane.

Low-Pressure Systems

WHEN the pressure reading on a barometer starts to fall, a low-pressure system may be on the way. Low-pressure systems bring most of the windiest weather. You can also expect long periods of overcast skies and rain.

Birth of a Low-Pressure System

Low-pressure systems usually start where warm air comes alongside colder air. This often happens when cold air from the Arctic moves south and meets warmer air moving north. A large volume of air with its own features of temperature and moisture is an **air mass**.

Different air masses do not mix easily, so there is a boundary line between them. This is called a **front**. Air can be moving in opposite directions on each side of the front. At first, the front is a straight or gently curving line. Then colder air starts to force its way beneath the warmer air. The warmer air starts to slide up over the colder air. The two types of air then begin to move in a spiral, and a wave forms in the front. This is the start of a low-pressure system.

Soon the cold air circles around behind the warmer air. Warm moist air is lifted up and cools to form cloud and rain.

The line in front of the warm air is called a **warm front**. The line in front of the advancing cold air is called a **cold front**. Eventually, the cold air catches up with the warm front to form an **occluded front**.

Diagram Notes
- Different types of air meet along a front.
- Air moves up along a front.
- The rising air cools and forms clouds.
- A band of clouds and rain can be expected along a front.

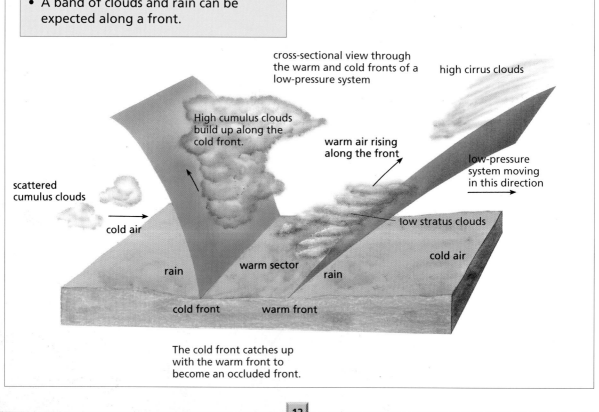

cross-sectional view through the warm and cold fronts of a low-pressure system

high cirrus clouds

High cumulus clouds build up along the cold front.

warm air rising along the front

low-pressure system moving in this direction

scattered cumulus clouds

cold air

low stratus clouds

cold air

rain

warm sector

rain

cold front

warm front

The cold front catches up with the warm front to become an occluded front.

Low-Pressure Systems on the Move

Low-pressure systems do not stay in the same place. They move in the direction of the main winds that blow across the earth. The main wind direction is called the **prevailing wind**. Prevailing winds vary with differences in latitude. The winds that blow around the equator are called trade winds.

Most low-pressure systems approach the Northen Hemisphere from the Atlantic Ocean where they pick up a large amount of moisture. Low-pressure systems also move towards the west coast of the United States and Canada from the Pacific Ocean.

A low-pressure area may be as big as 1 million square miles, but most are much smaller. They bring types of weather that can usually be predicted.

As the warm front approaches, clouds become lower until there is continuous rain. The wind increases and changes direction to the south. After the rain belt, there may be a short period of warmer weather in the **warm sector**. This is followed by more clouds and rain, as the cold front passes by. After the cold front, the winds are blustery with scattered showers. As the low-pressure system moves away, the winds become lighter again.

Some of the coldest weather in the North America is brought by low-pressure systems. Very cold air from the Arctic is sucked down by the spiral of air around the system. The weather feels even colder because the wind blows strongly.

The weather from some low-pressure systems is not always predicted so accurately. Low-pressure systems do not always move either at the speed or in the exact direction that is forecast. In 1987, one very severe low-pressure system came unexpectedly across the southern part of Great Britain. It was one of the worst **storms** this century.

DID YOU KNOW? ?

Bands of strong winds called jet streams circle the atmosphere at a high level. These provide the trigger that helps low-pressure systems to form.

Photo Notes
- Satellite image of a low-pressure system passing over Great Britain.
- Air is spinning in toward the center of the system.
- Clouds forms along the fronts between warm and cold air.

Gales and Storms

Strong winds are a danger to people and their property. High-sided trucks can be blown over by winds at little more than 50 miles per hour. Stronger winds are able to uproot tall trees with shallow roots. Buildings are also at risk, especially their chimneys and roof tiles.

Along coastlines, strong winds make powerful waves that batter sea defenses. These are good reasons why weather reports about gales and storms have to be taken seriously.

The Beaufort Scale

Weather forecasts usually give the wind speed in miles per hour or in **knots**. Wind speed is also given using the **Beaufort scale**. Wind on this scale is given as a figure from 0 to 12. A gale force wind starts at force 8 when the wind has reached 32 miles per hour. There are different strengths of gale until the wind rises above 63 miles per hour when it becomes a storm.

After about 74 miles per hour, a storm becomes a hurricane. Gales and storms usually come with a low-pressure system. The winds become stronger where the isobars are close together near the center of the low-pressure system. Sometimes there is a sudden **gust** of wind, when the wind speed increases for a short time. A sudden gust can do more damage in a few seconds than wind at a lower speed that blows for longer. Damage by the wind is often made worse when rivers and the sea are made to overflow and flood.

Photo Notes

- A brick wall blown over during the 1987 storm in southern England.
- Buildings and trees survived, but weak cement in the wall gave way.
- Walls that collapse can cause great damage and injuries.

Storm Damage

Gales and storms sweep across the country several times each year. Most of them are predicted, so people are warned in advance. When this happens, the best advice is to stay indoors.

One of the most damaging storms this century struck Great Britain in October 1987. Weather forecasters thought it would miss Britain, but it moved further north and swept across southern England. The winds came as part of a very deep low-pressure system that moved in from the Atlantic. It was called "deep" because the pressure at its center was very low. At one stage, the pressure at the center was only 956 millibars. This is about 30 millibars below the average low-pressure system.

Winds reached an average speed of 70 miles per hour with gusts at 104 miles per hour. About 15 million trees were uprooted in southern England. They fell on cars, houses, and power cables. They blocked roads and railroad lines.

In January, November, and December 1993 there were more gale and storm force winds in Great Britain, as deep low-pressure systems moved across the country. On one day in January, six people were killed; four died in road accidents, and two were crushed in their car by a falling tree.

The cost of the damage was counted in millions of dollars. Fewer trees were uprooted during these storms. Many of the weaker ones had already been uprooted in 1987.

A problem is that these kinds of winds do not come very often to this part of the world. Buildings and trees can survive for years, but when a storm does come, any weakness is suddenly exposed. Driving conditions become too dangerous for safety, but many people still try to carry on as if nothing is happening. Sometimes, perhaps, people should have a little more respect for nature's power.

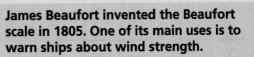

DID YOU KNOW? [?]

James Beaufort invented the Beaufort scale in 1805. One of its main uses is to warn ships about wind strength.

Cloudbursts

WEEKS of hot weather can come to a sudden end when the sky seems to open and every drop of rain in the clouds falls at once. It happens quickly with quite frightening results. Drains cannot cope and roads are soon covered in sheets of water. Rivers can rise and burst their banks within a very short time. This is a time when accidents are bound to happen.

Cumulonimbus Clouds

The heaviest rain falls from dark storm clouds called **cumulonimbus** clouds. Cumulonimbus clouds are easy to recognize. They billow out like great balls of cotton wool and grow up to 8 miles high. At the top, the cloud flattens out in the shape of an anvil or tomahawk. A cumulonimbus cloud grows as moist air is lifted up in a thermal from the warm ground or a warm sea.

Cloud and rain droplets form around tiny particles of salt, dust, pollen, and sometimes pieces from volcanic eruptions. Raindrops become larger as they collide with each other. Currents in a cumulonimbus cloud keep the droplets moving up and down, growing larger all the time. Eventually, there is a **cloudburst** when the air is no longer able to keep the raindrops in the air.

Hailstones are large lumps of frozen water that sometimes fall from cumulonimbus clouds. They form when droplets of rain and snow rise and fall many times in a cloud. As they move, they collide and join with very cold water droplets. They fall as hail when they become too heavy to stay in the air. They vary from less than an inch to 5 inches across, though much larger ones have fallen. Some have even killed people.

Photo Notes
- Cumulonimbus clouds build up to great heights.
- The aircraft is flying into the cloud to measure the temperature and other conditions inside it.
- Freezing rain, lightning, and strong winds can make this work dangerous.

Photo Notes
- The village of Vaison-La-Romaine in southeast France.
- Downpours over several days in September 1993 caused rivers to flood.
- Too much rain fell in too short a time for the rivers to cope.

Downpours of Rain

A cloudburst happens suddenly and may last for only a few minutes. In that time, over 4 inches of rain can fall. That is longer than your longest finger. On one day in February 1993, 5 inches of rain fell on Darwin in Australia's Northern Territory.

In the same month on the island of Java, 13 inches of rain fell in only two and a half days. Giant clouds had built up in tropical low-pressure areas. Because February is one of the hottest months of the year in these areas, the amount of evaporation and uplift is greatest then.

Also in 1993, there were summer downpours in parts of Europe. In June, 1.7 inches of rain fell in one day on the Spanish town of Albacete. Near Augsburg in Germany, there was 3.4 inches, 2.4 inches, then 2.3 inches of rain in three days running. Toward the end of the summer, heavy rain brought serious flooding throughout countries in southern Europe.

There is a special problem with rainfall over several days. Soil becomes water-logged and no more rain can sink into it.

Any more rain then has to run off the surface and into the rivers. This causes a **flash flood** that overflows the banks and flows over fields and through towns and villages at great speed.

Sudden downpours often lead to road accidents. Windshield wipers cannot clear the rain fast enough for a driver to see the car in front. Standing water on the road makes it hard to stop in time. The brakes go on, but the tires skid over the water instead of coming in contact with the road. This is **hydroplaning**. Motorists need to drive slowly and carefully; better still, they should pull over and wait until the rain stops. It is impossible to forecast exactly when and where a downpour will happen. People need to take great care when they see cumulonimbus clouds.

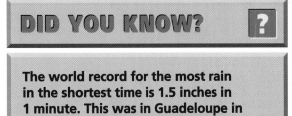

DID YOU KNOW?

The world record for the most rain in the shortest time is 1.5 inches in 1 minute. This was in Guadeloupe in Central America.

Thunder and Lightning

THE chances of being hit by **lightning** are very small. Yet, every year, people are killed by either a direct hit or something that has been hit falling on them. In the United States, about 100 people are killed by lightning each year. Many people who are hit by lightning do survive.

An Electric Spark

Lightning is a giant electric spark. We see this as a **flash** that lasts for about a fifth (0.2) of a second. The flash can be between a cloud and the ground or it can be from the ground up to the cloud. This gives the jagged lines of **streaked** or **forked lightning**. Lightning can also be from the top to the bottom of a cloud. This is often seen as **sheet lightning**.

Photo Notes
- Lightning from a thundercloud over Tucson, Arizona.
- Each flash is made of many strokes that make the lightning seem to flicker.
- Lightning causes deaths, damage to buildings, and forest fires.

Scientists disagree on what causes lightning. The flash must occur between something that has a negative electrical charge and something that has a positive electrical charge. One explanation is that ice particles in a cloud become negatively charged. The ground and the top of a cloud are positively charged. The negative charge first jumps toward the positive charge as a **stroke**. This is called a **leader stroke**. A **return stroke** goes back up the same path and causes the shock waves we hear as **thunder**.

Many different strokes make up a flash of lightning. We see these different strokes as a flicker of lightning. Enormous amounts of energy are released by lightning.

Great heat along the strokes makes the air suddenly expand. This is what we hear as thunder. We are likely to see the lightning before we hear the thunder because light travels much faster than sound.

Lightning Strikes

In the United States, there are more than a million flashes of lightning every year. They can happen in any month though they are more common in the warmer summer months. Most cause no damage at all. The few that do are able to kill, damage, and set fire to trees and buildings. Lightning costs electric companies millions of dollars each year when power cables are struck.

People in open fields are most at risk from being hit by lightning. There is also a risk in taking shelter under a tree or anything else that could fall.

Lightning is attracted to pointed pieces of metal, no matter how small. Police in Great Britain were at risk when they wore hard hats with metal spikes on top. People on sports fields are sometimes hit, especially if they are wearing or carrying something made of metal. In October 1993, a golfer was lucky to survive when his umbrella was hit. Two days later, a schoolboy was killed on a sports field. People inside a building are not completely safe. Lightning can come into a room through a gap or down a chimney. In September 1993, one person was hit while in the kitchen.

A building can be protected by a **lightning conductor**. A conductor brings the lightning down to ground along a wire without causing damage to the building. If you are outside, it is safest to lie down flat so that you do not make a high point for the lightning to hit. Another option is to crouch down so that, if you are struck, electricity can get to the ground without passing through your heart or head. People wearing thick rubber soles have some chance of surviving. You are also likely to be safe in a car. The electricity passes around the car's metal body then jumps safely to the ground.

Lightning starts bush and forest fires that can quickly spread and cause great damage to vegetation, wildlife, and property. Dry grass is easily set fire and winds soon fan and spread the flames. About 75,000 forest fires are thought to be started by lightning in the United States every year. Places in Australia and Africa where there is a seasonal drought are also affected by fires started by lightning.

DID YOU KNOW? [?]

One of the worst disasters caused by lightning occurred in Ireland in 1697. Lightning hit Athlone Castle. The ammunition store was hit and most of the castle was blown up.

Photo Notes
- A bush fire in Australia's Northern Territory.
- Lightning set fire to dry grassland and trees.
- Winds fanned the flames and spread the fires.

Hurricanes

TROPICAL storm can cause more damage to the largest area in a short time than any other type of weather. In some parts of the world, there is a high risk that a tropical storm will strike several times during a person's life. It is a risk that many people seem prepared to take.

Hurricane Features

Tropical storms are known by many names, depending on where they occur. They are called *hurricanes* in the Atlantic Ocean, *typhoons* in the southwest part of the Pacific Ocean, and *cyclones* in the Indian Ocean. They are called *willy-willies* when they blow south over the northern part of Australia and nearby islands. There are no real differences among them. One unusual feature of a hurricane is the small area in the center, where the air is calm. This is the **eye** of the hurricane.

A hurricane has all the same features as a low-pressure system, but all the features are more extreme. Hurricane force winds start at 75 miles per hour and can go up to over 200 miles per hour. It is an area where there is very low pressure at the center. Winds swirl toward the eye at the center, then rise upward.

The air swirling around the eye holds a lot of moisture, which forms a dense wall of thunderclouds. These can rise to 6 miles. The whole hurricane is less than one quarter the size of a low-pressure system.

Diagram Notes
- A very intense area of low pressure is called a hurricane.
- Winds are sucked toward the center, then flow upward at great speed.
- Hurricanes form in tropical areas over warm oceans.
- They move in an erratic curving path for about two weeks until they die out.

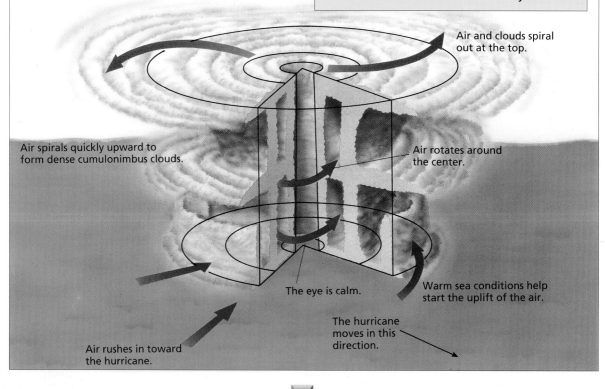

Air and clouds spiral out at the top.

Air spirals quickly upward to form dense cumulonimbus clouds.

Air rotates around the center.

The eye is calm.

Warm sea conditions help start the uplift of the air.

Air rushes in toward the hurricane.

The hurricane moves in this direction.

Hurricane Heat

An enormous amount of energy is needed to start a hurricane and keep it going. Heat from the sun gives this energy. This is why hurricanes mainly start at certain times of the year. In the northern hemisphere, they start when heat from the sun is greatest toward the middle of the year. They become more common from August to October when the heat has built up over several months. In the southern hemisphere, they form from December to May for the same reason.

Hurricanes start over warm oceans. The water temperature at the surface needs to be at least 80° F before a hurricane can start. A large amount of water is evaporated, then starts to rise. Air flowing out at high levels may help to start this. The rising air begins to move in an upward spiral. More air rushes in at the base to replace it. Vast amounts of water are kept in the clouds as the uplift of air continues. Energy is released as the water vapor condenses to form clouds and rain.

There are several hurricanes in different parts of the world every year. There are usually about six in the North Atlantic, though they do not all reach land. Each hurricane is given a name. For many years, only female names were used. Now both male and female names are used.

Recent hurricanes have included typhoons Kina and Nina that hit Fiji and the Solomon Islands in January 1993. About 15 people were killed and 20,000 were made homeless. In August 1994, Typhoon Fred swept onto the mainland of China killing about 800 people. Even this was very few compared to the thousands and sometimes tens of thousands who have died during typhoons and cyclones in southeast Asia over the last 50 years.

DID YOU KNOW? [?]

In one week of September 1993, four hurricanes affected different parts of the world at once. Typhoons "Abe" and "Becky" passed through the Philippines and South China Sea. Hurricanes "Lidia" and "Gert" moved over parts of Central America.

Hurricane Tracks

The best way to prevent damage from any of nature's forces is usually to predict when and where they will happen. Weather satellites now watch hurricanes as they start and follow them as they move. They even give information about where they might start. The problem is that it is still very difficult to predict exactly where they will go or how fast they will move. Each hurricane is different.

The Average Hurricane

Hurricanes do behave in some ways that can be predicted. They usually start over warm sea areas, in places between 5° and 25° latitude north or south of the equator. They start to move at about 6 miles per hour and become faster until they are traveling at about 19 miles per hour. After about a week, their strength has mostly gone, and they slow down again. They lose their energy more quickly when they move over land. Friction from the ground and the loss of warm, moist air causes them to do this.

Hurricanes in each part of the world usually move in the same general direction. They move in a broad curve in the same direction as the prevailing winds. Some swing quite sharply in the later part of their course.

Hurricanes from the Atlantic Ocean move northwest over the Caribbean Sea and the Gulf of Mexico. They often veer to the northeast as they reach the mainland, though some carry on inland and die out.

Some hurricanes cross the Atlantic Ocean and reach Europe. They become weaker the further they travel. In September 1993, the remains of Hurricane Floyd reached the northwest coast of France. The winds were still gusting at 99 miles per hour with the pressure at 982 millibars.

In the Pacific and Indian Oceans, typhoons and cyclones move in the same kind of way. The direction depends on whether the hurricane is north or south of the equator.

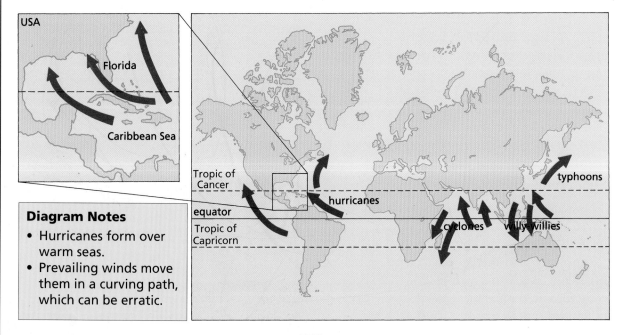

Diagram Notes
- Hurricanes form over warm seas.
- Prevailing winds move them in a curving path, which can be erratic.

Hurricane Planning

Hurricanes are small weather features. They measure only about 250 miles to 375 miles across. They move over oceans that are thousands of miles wide. Their small size concentrates all their energy on the few places where they happen to cross. It also means they pass by other places and leave them undamaged.

A hurricane's curving course is hard to predict. Its speed and track can change when it moves over land then change again if it moves back over the sea. It is like a spinning top that is out of control. This is what makes it very hard to give a proper warning about where a hurricane will strike. People do not like to move out of their homes when there is a chance that a forecast might be wrong.

People who live around the Gulf of Mexico, in states such as Florida and Texas, are well organized in case of a hurricane. A hurricane watch announcement is given if there is any chance that one will arrive. A hurricane warning is given when one is certain to arrive within 24 hours. This is when people must decide whether to stay in their homes, go to a hurricane shelter, or get out of the area.

There are basic rules about what to do in the event of a hurricane. Windows need to be taped to stop the glass from being shattered. Loose garden furniture needs to be tied down, or perhaps put in the house.

Water needs to be kept in secure containers and in a bathtub, as the supplies may be cut off after the hurricane. A flashlight, with batteries that work, is needed in case power lines are cut. Sleeping bags, food, water, and special medicines need to be brought to the hurricane shelter.

DID YOU KNOW?

During a hurricane, it is best to stay in one place. It is especially dangerous to go outside when the calm of the eye arrives. It will not last for long. When the hurricane is over, go back to your home, but continue to be careful. Gas pipes may be broken and electricity cables may be lying on the ground. If you are lucky, there may be a house left to go home to.

Photo Notes
- Signs help people evacuate from this area of Florida before a hurricane arrives.
- Many homes and other buildings are not strong enough to survive 200 mph winds.
- There is a risk of traffic jams if evacuations are not well planned and there is not enough warning time.

Hurricane Andrew

FLORIDA is well known for sunshine and vacations. Millions of visitors from here and other countries go to visit its beaches and other attractions. Miami is one of the main tourist resorts in the country. It is also where all our space flights are launched. Florida gets another kind of visitor from time to time. This comes in the unwelcome shape of a hurricane. Hurricane Andrew arrived for a short time in 1992.

Andrew Is Born

This hurricane began in the same way that most hurricanes begin. Halfway through August, rising air over the Atlantic Ocean began to take shape as a tropical storm. Satellites watched its progress as it started to move east. For awhile, it looked as if it might not get any more powerful. Then it seemed to change its mind.

By the sixth day, the winds had reached the critical limit of 75 miles per hour. It was now a hurricane called Andrew.

Twelve hours later, the winds had risen to over 150 miles per hour. Andrew moved over the Bahamas where its wind speed dropped to 140 miles per hour. It moved on toward Florida, and the wind speed rose again. The hurricane traveled at about 19 miles per hour toward the Florida peninsula. By then everybody knew it was coming. It roared across flat land in the southern tip of Florida then continued east over the Gulf of Mexico. Two days later, it hit the mainland in Louisiana. This was nine days after it had started. Then, like other hurricanes, it quickly lost its strength over land and died out.

Photo Notes
- Coastal areas are badly affected by hurricane damage.
- Violent winds and a sea surge lift the sea level and cause flooding.
- The cost of damage to property is enormous in a built-up area such as Florida.

Lessons from Andrew

Hurricane Andrew is said to be the third worst hurricane to reach the mainland of North America this century. By the time it died out, it had left 65 people dead and made 160,000 people homeless. The cost of the damage was about $30 billion.

The wind speed became impossible to measure. It broke the anemometer at the weather station.

Wind speed was probably about 143 miles per hour with gusts that may have reached 200 miles per hour. The trail of damage it left was 25 miles across, though most of the worst damage was done along a much smaller track.

The low pressure caused the sea to rise by almost 16 feet. Boats in the marinas were picked up and thrown ashore. The waves and current tore coral and sponges off the ocean bed. Buildings along the coast were swamped.

About 80,000 homes were completely wrecked by the winds. Another 55,000 were left with serious damage. Mobile homes that were used as vacation and permanent homes were blown apart. The wood they were built from shattered and caused more damage.

Photo Notes
- Mobile homes were completely wrecked by the 200 miles per hour gusts of wind that came in Hurricane Andrew.
- The hurricane crossed the southern part of Florida in August 1992.
- Wood shattered into dangerous flying splinters.
- Homes like these may not be a good idea in an area that suffers from hurricanes.

In Louisiana, over 690,000 acres of mangrove forest and swamp land were destroyed. Mud and organic material were disturbed; this used up oxygen in the water. About 182 million fish died from lack of oxygen.

About 25,000 people have now left the area and do not intend to come back. Others have stayed and are trying to make up what they have lost.

One way to save lives is for more people to evacuate the area. A problem with this idea is that if there was less than 24 hours' notice, there could be a traffic jam throughout Florida. Tourists and residents would all be caught up in the jam. If a hurricane hit a traffic jam, the death toll could be counted in thousands. Perhaps the best answer is to make sure that buildings are stronger and that windows have shutters. There seems to be no way that everyone can be made safe.

DID YOU KNOW? ?

Before Hurricane Andrew, regulations in this part of Florida said that buildings had to be able to survive in 118 miles per hour winds. It seems as if these regulations will need to be changed.

Asian Cyclones

NOWHERE are so many deaths caused by tropical storms than in the countries that have a shoreline on the Indian Ocean. Two countries are especially at risk. To the east is Bangladesh and to the west is Pakistan. These are two of the world's poorest countries. Cyclones and the sea flooding that they have brought with them have played a large part in keeping the people poor.

The Danger Zone

Cyclones form over the warm seawater of the Indian Ocean. When they start to move, they go in a northwesterly direction toward the Asian mainland.

Photo Notes
- Survivors from a cyclone that flooded part of Bangladesh in 1990.
- Homes have been smashed and people's property has been washed away.

Cyclones to the east of India move over the Bay of Bengal as they approach Bangladesh. This is where the Ganges and Brahmaputra rivers flow out to the sea.

Most of Bangladesh is low-lying land, built up from mud washed down by the great rivers. The mud forms low islands that are never more than a few feet above sea level. There is no higher land on any of them. The islands grow every year as more mud is washed down in the rivers.

As a cyclone approaches the land, the winds build up giant waves in the Bay of Bengal. As the bay becomes more narrow, the waves are pushed up even higher. During one cyclone in 1985, waves up to 20 feet high swept over the low delta islands. Thousands of people were swept away and drowned.

Poverty Kills

Millions of people in Bangladesh live on the low delta islands. Bangladesh is one of the world's poorest and most crowded countries. The population is increasing by about two million people every year. Most of the people live by farming. Poverty forces many of them to live on any piece of land they can farm, no matter how dangerous it is. Land in the delta has only just been formed by the mud. There are no good defenses to stop strong waves sweeping over the islands.

Cyclones can be seen by satellites, but it is not always easy to get this information to everyone. Hardly anyone owns a TV set, many do not have a radio, and few can even afford a newspaper. Even with the right information, there is still not much that the people can do. There is little higher ground to which they can escape, and there is no quick way to get off the islands in an emergency.

The result is that every few years there is another cyclone and flood disaster. There were at least five major disasters between 1960 and 1970. In 1985, about 500,000 people were killed. Then in 1990, two cyclones hit the same place in one month.

Despite storm warnings and cyclone shelters, about 166 people were killed in the first cyclone, and at least 140,000 were killed during the second. Crops and animals were also wiped out, and the survivors lost the few things they owned.

Every time there is a cyclone disaster, aid money is sent and the government tries to help the survivors. But little is done to stop the problem from happening again. Some hurricane shelters are built, but people need stronger homes. The population continues to rise, so the pressure on both land and other resources is increased.

This is a part of the world where living with frequent disasters has turned millions of people into bare survivors. The problem is a huge one, and it will be a very long time before this situation is likely to change.

DID YOU KNOW? ?

The population of Bangladesh in 1980 was 88 million. By the year 2000, it will have reached more than 150 million.

Great Twisters

I N November 1993, a farmer in Wales reported that the wind had picked up some of his sheep and moved them into another field. There was a river and a stone wall in the way so they could not have walked. Nobody saw the flying sheep, but the story is not impossible. A **tornado** had been seen heading for the field, ripping off shed roofs on the way. The sheep might have been its next victims. Stories about flying animals are not all that unusual. Frogs and snails have been reported as falling from the sky. The cause of this was probably also a tornado.

Whirlpools of Air

A tornado is a violent whirling column of air. They are also called **twisters**. They can cause more damage than a hurricane, but over a much smaller area.

A tornado has some things in common with low-pressure systems and hurricanes. They are all areas with low pressure at the center, the air spirals around the center, and it also spirals upward. Unlike low-pressure systems and hurricanes, tornadoes are much smaller and the winds around them are far stronger.

Most tornadoes are only a few hundred feet across. The wind races around the center at speeds of about 500 miles per hour. Air is lifted up at about 150 miles per hour.

A curved column of rising air stretches from the ground to the base of a cloud as it moves across the landscape. The curve is caused by friction from the ground that drags the base behind the rest of the column. Predicting where one will go next is almost impossible.

Photo Notes
- A tornado in Kansas.
- A curved column of rotating air reaches from the ground to the base of a giant thundercloud.
- Warm, moist air is being sucked up toward cold air at low pressure.

Why Tornadoes Form

Tornadoes start to form along a front between warm, moist air and cold, dry air. This can happen at any time of year. The conditions are most suitable when a deep low-pressure system moves quickly across the land, bringing cold air in contact with warmer air. No one knows for sure how many tornadoes occur each year, because many of the storms occur where there are not a lot of people. Tornadoes in these areas may not be reported. About 700 tornadoes have been reported each year in the United States since the middle of the 1950s.

In the United States, flat land and extreme temperatures make conditions ideal for tornadoes. They come mostly in spring and summer when the difference between warm, moist air and cool, dry air can be greatest. The warm air moves north over the Great Plains from the Gulf of Mexico. It wedges in beneath the colder air along a front. Warm air starts to rise up toward the colder air. An eddy is started, which starts to suck in more air at ground level. The spiral becomes faster until a narrow upward column of air is formed.

Dense clouds form in the column as the moist air condenses on the way up. The cloud can take on different colors, depending on what type of soil it picks up.

The tornado moves in an irregular manner. Sometimes the base touches the ground. At other times, it skips over ground in a series of short hops.

A similar feature can form over water. This is called a **waterspout**. The pillar of spinning air sucks up water instead of soil and debris. Small boats in its way can also be sucked up. Some boats have been sunk when tons of water have been dumped on them. The best idea is to steer clear of where you think it might be going.

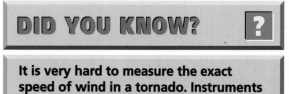

DID YOU KNOW? **?**

It is very hard to measure the exact speed of wind in a tornado. Instruments set up to measure it are usually broken by the strength of the wind.

Tornado Alley

TORNADOES are not unusual in the Great Plains and the Midwest. They vary in size and strength, but all of them are dangerous. About 90 people are killed by tornadoes every year. The cost of their damage is counted in millions of dollars.

Photo Notes

- Tornado damage in the state of Georgia.
- It left a narrow trail of damage, completely destroying a street of houses.
- Strong wind and the difference in air pressure caused the damage.

States at Risk

Tornadoes can strike anywhere from west to east between the Rocky Mountains and Illinois, and north to south between Canada and New Mexico, Texas, and Alabama. Tornadoes come every year and sometimes many times in one day. This is particularly true in the Great Plains region, which is why it is known as "Tornado Alley."

Tornadoes leave a terrible trail of death and damage. In November 1989, one tornado killed 14 people in Alabama. In August 1990, 25 people were killed further north in Illinois. Then in 1991, 25 people died when a tornado struck a trailer park in Kansas. The trailers and the people in them stood no chance.

The worst damage on record was from a giant tornado that started in Missouri in March 1925. The twisting column of air grew to become 1 mile across. It moved across the landscape at 40 miles per hour. Everything in its path was flattened. Four towns were completely wrecked, and six others were badly damaged. There were 689 deaths, 1,980 injuries, and 11,000 people were left homeless. The tornado traveled 217 miles before it finally died out in Illinois. There has been nothing like it since then, but there is no reason to think that there will not be another one of the same size.

Tornado Power

Tornadoes do part of the damage by the speed and strength of the wind. Any building has to be extremely strong to survive winds of 500 miles per hour. Flying debris causes more damage. Anything that is not fixed to the ground is likely to be picked up and thrown around. Roofs are ripped off by the upward blast of air. Cars and other vehicles are blown over and tossed about. People and animals caught in the open are blown away.

Damage to buildings is also caused by the very low air pressure inside the tornado. Air rushes from the normal pressure inside a building to the tornado's low-pressure area. The sudden difference in air pressure makes the building explode as the walls, doors, windows, and roof are all blown out.

As with all types of natural disaster, people find ways to cope with the risk. Weather forecasters watch for conditions that make it likely that tornadoes will form. Tornadoes are followed on radar and by ground reports. Radio warnings are given so people can expect the worst.

In places where tornadoes often strike, schoolchildren have practice drills so they know what to do. If there is a direct hit on a building, nowhere is safe except underground in a basement. People caught out in the open have a chance of surviving if they lie down in a ditch. The tornado can pass overhead without touching the ground at all. It may even jump away in a different direction.

One fear is that the number of tornadoes has been increasing. In the 20 years up to 1950, there were about 160 tornadoes every year. This rose to 580 over the next 20 years. The figure is now about 1,000. It may be that recordkeeping for tornadoes has improved. The increase could also be due to a change in the climate or the surface of the ground, or both.

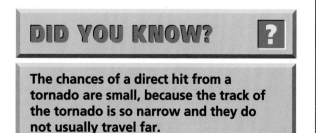

DID YOU KNOW? ?

The chances of a direct hit from a tornado are small, because the track of the tornado is so narrow and they do not usually travel far.

Sunburn

People need some sunshine. It helps make vitamin D that is needed to produce calcium for healthy bones. Besides, a vacation in the sun is far more enjoyable than a vacation spent in the rain. But like too much of any type of weather, too much sunshine can bring problems. People's health is at risk from too much exposure to the sun.

Beware of the Sun

Weather forecasts in summer now give advice on how long it is safe to stay out in the sun. Getting **sunstroke** is one problem. This is also called **heatstroke**. People who are not used to strong sun are especially at risk. Sunstroke can ruin a vacation for several days. An extreme case of sunstroke can kill.

Another problem with too much exposure to the sun is **skin cancer**. Energy from the sun is also called **radiation**.

One form of radiation is called UVB, which is a type of ultraviolet radiation. It burns and damages the skin. Bad damage can become a **malignant melanoma**, which is a form of skin cancer. A cancer can spread rapidly through the body and destroy what it affects. Skin cancer can start in a small way. A natural mole on the skin can be damaged first. If the damage is not noticed in time, it can start to spread. Nothing may happen for many years before the problem suddenly begins. Damage to the skin when a person is young may not have an effect until he or she is much older.

Photo Notes
- Sunbathing on a beach in Queensland, Australia.
- Most people enjoy being in the sun, but strong sunshine burns the skin and can cause skin cancer.
- The cancer can start in children but not develop until many years later.
- Babies, children, and adults are all at risk.

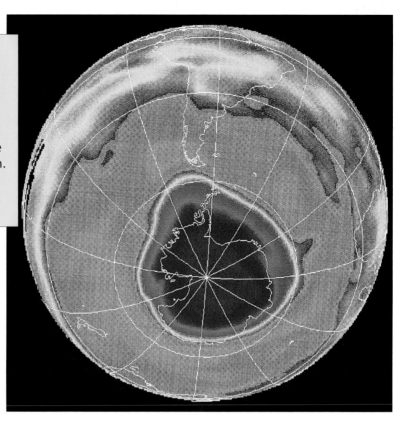

Photo Notes
- The ozone hole over the Antarctic in 1990.
- The violet and pink areas show where ozone has been destroyed and harmful ultraviolet radiation from the sun is able to get to the earth.
- Scientists believe the ozone layer is being destroyed by chemicals.

Slip, Slop, Slap

The sun's radiation passes through a layer of gases in the upper part of the atmosphere called the **ozone layer**. Ozone is a gas that filters out much of the harmful ultraviolet radiation that causes sunburn and leads to skin cancer. This layer is being destroyed by chemicals that people use and release into the air. One group of chemicals is CFCs (chlorofluorocarbons). These are used in aerosol sprays and other products. The CFCs destroy the molecules of ozone in the ozone layer.

Scientists talk about **ozone holes** to show that this layer is being destroyed. At first, the ozone holes were identified over Antarctica. Now the holes seem to be growing and spreading to other places. In the United States, there are now about 34,000 new cases of melanoma every year. Many of these are caused by too much exposure to the sun. About 1,200 people die each year because of skin cancer. Yet only one in five people uses sunblock and one in two uses nothing at all. Fewer than one in ten people wear a hat or shirt to protect themselves against the sun.

In Australia, where many people are fair-skinned and the sun is very hot, the risk of skin cancer is much greater than in other parts of the world. This is why there is now a "Slip, slop, slap" campaign. People are advised to slip on a shirt, slop on some sunblock, and slap on a hat. A new rule in some Australian schools is "no hat, no play."

People will have to be more careful about enjoying the sunshine in the future. Skin needs to be protected by clothes or strong sunblock. Harmful radiation may also affect crops and animals. Use of CFCs is banned in many countries, but damage to the ozone layer has already been done.

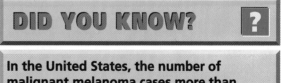

DID YOU KNOW? ?

In the United States, the number of malignant melanoma cases more than doubled between 1980 and 1995. More people know about the dangers, but many still ignore the advice to protect themselves.

Drought on the Land

PEOPLE everywhere depend on water. We all need to drink and to use it in many other ways. Farmers need it to grow crops and to raise animals. Many farmers live off the food they grow, so their whole way of life depends on water. In some countries, a constant supply of water is taken for granted. Not everyone is so lucky.

Patterns of Rainfall

About 34 inches of rain and other forms of precipitation fall to the earth annually. Some regions of the earth have a much heavier rainfall and others get much less rain. Some regions near the equator have received as much as 400 inches of rain a year. But other tropical regions receive very little rain.

The patterns of rainfall in the United States vary greatly. In Death Valley, California, less than 2 inches of rain falls each year. But the northwest coastal states can expect up to 150 inches a year. People in the United States do not expect a shortage of water because dams and reservoirs have been built. There is a much greater difference in rainfall between the seasons in some parts of the world.

In a monsoon climate, the wind blows from the land for about six months then from the sea for the other six months. This brings dry weather followed by months of wet weather. A period of dry weather in which there may be no rain at all is called a **drought**. In a wet month, 14 inches of rain might fall. Farmers in monsoon areas use special methods to make the best of the regular wet and dry seasons. Crops will grow well as long as the monsoon rains arrive on time.

Photo Notes

- A field of sugar beet in Great Britain during the 1976 drought.
- The sugar beet in the background is healthy because water is escaping from a drain under the soil.
- Crops fail, but people do not starve when this happens.
- There is enough money to buy food from other countries.

Causes of Drought

Drought conditions usually come in summer when a large area of high pressure spreads over an area and does not move. The air is calm and hot enough to keep all its moisture in the form of water vapor. Air is sinking instead of rising, so clouds do not form. These were the conditions that brought drought to the Midwest, northern Great Plains, and parts of the Southeast in 1988. California had a serious drought for most of the 1980s. In the summer of 1993, while the Midwest was drenched with rain, the South was almost rainless.

A drought ends in one of two main ways: when heat builds up over the land and starts thunderstorms, or when the high–pressure area either drifts away or is forced away by a low-pressure system. It is usually several years before there is another long dry period.

An annual drought can be expected in areas with a **savannah** climate. This type of climate exists in areas between the deserts and the tropical rain forests. In Africa, countries such as Mali, Chad, Sudan, and Angola all have this type of climate. The northern parts of Australia and parts of Brazil have a similar climate.

Rain comes when the sun is at its highest and the heat is greatest. Heat makes air rise and form clouds. Rain sometimes comes from these clouds, though sometimes it does not. There may be a heavy shower of rain in one place, but none at all somewhere nearby.

High temperatures mean that much of the rainwater is quickly evaporated again.

It is very hard to predict what the rainfall will be from year to year in an area with a savannah climate. Years of extreme drought seem to be followed by wetter years, then more drought years return. In 1993, drought conditions came back to northeast Brazil. The area has a long history of droughts.

DID YOU KNOW? **?**

The Great Plains had one of the worst droughts in its history from 1931 to 1938. The whole country suffered as food became scarce and prices went up.

When the Rains Fail

PEOPLE are affected by drought in different ways. In developed countries, reservoirs usually have enough water to keep everyone supplied with most of their needs. Farmers lose some of their crops, but they can benefit if a shortage causes prices to go up. In poorer countries, the effects are often much more serious. Rivers and waterholes dry up. Crops fail, and animals die of thirst. At its worst, drought can lead to **famine** that affects millions of people.

The Effects of Drought

A drought in the United States may be welcomed at first. It is unusual to have several weeks without rain, so people start to enjoy the sun. But problems soon start to develop. Reservoirs run low, and water departments put restrictions on how much water can be used. They often urge people not to water their lawns or wash their cars.

Buildings can crack during a drought because the ground dries out and starts to shrink. Crops fail, but at least nobody dies or starves because of the drought.

Rainfall in the central part of the United States and in parts of Australia is normally low and can be unreliable. Soil can dry out and be blown away under these conditions. This is called **soil erosion**. In the 1930s, soil erosion by the wind affected so many states that the area was called the "Dust Bowl." Farmers now are more careful about how they use the land. There is always the danger that another drought could have the same effect.

> **Photo Notes**
> - Drought in New South Wales in Australia.
> - The ground dries out and grass cannot grow.
> - Sheep and cattle on large ranches cannot find water or food.

Photo Notes
- Planting trees in Burkina Faso.
- Burkina Faso is on the southern edge of the Sahara Desert.
- Land has been overgrazed and has turned to desert.
- Trees help keep moisture in the soil and make it fertile when leaves fall and rot.
- Some trees give food and other products that help people survive.

Famine Strikes

Problems from droughts in poor countries have become more common in recent years. Countries in Africa have been hit the hardest. In the 1970s, there were droughts in countries to the south of the Sahara Desert. This area is called the Sahel. In the 1980s and into the 1990s, the rains failed to come to Ethiopia, Somalia, and other African countries. These are some of the world's poorest countries and some of the world's poorest people. Crops failed and animals died. This brought disaster to people whose only way of making a living is farming. There were widespread famines, and thousands of people died.

In some countries, the problem of drought has been made worse by war and by the ways that people have changed the environment. Trees have been cut down, and too many animals have been grazed on the land. Without trees and grass, heavy rain soon washes the soil away. Vegetation also gives the shade that helps the soil maintain more of its moisture. Crops cannot be grown in dry, eroded soil. This makes problems of drought even worse.

Aid has often come too late to save people from starvation and disease. Yet satellites are able to see that crops are failing long before a famine starts. Money is spent on emergency food aid, but there is also a need to think about the future. More needs to be done to stop soil from being washed away and being overused. Trees need to be planted and better ways found to store water. Spending aid money in these ways could do much to help overcome the problems of drought in the future.

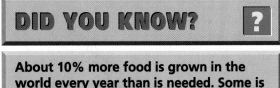

DID YOU KNOW? **?**

About 10% more food is grown in the world every year than is needed. Some is thrown away or stored to keep prices up. A little is given as food aid in flood, earthquake, famine, and other emergencies.

Fogbound

Fog leads to some of the worst traffic accidents on American roads. Too many drivers think that they can drive through **fog** at high speed and still be able to brake in time to avoid the car in front of them. If one motorist makes a mistake and crashes, the cars behind come to a stop only when they bump into each other.

Conditions for Fog

Fog forms when water vapor in the air is cooled and turns into tiny cloud droplets. In Great Britain, where fog is a common sight, this happens when warm moist air moves north over land that is cold. The air cools down, and its water vapor condenses to give fog. Calm conditions are needed for fog to form.

Autumn is the time of year when fog is most common. This is when warm moist air often blows north over a land that is cooling rapidly after the summer. In winter, **freezing fog** forms when moist air is cooled to even lower temperatures. Fog usually forms during the night when the temperature is lowest.

River valleys and other areas of sheltered lowland are ideal places for fog to form. Cold air drains down into these areas during the night. Moist air condenses to give a thick pocket of fog. Motorists driving in clear sunlight can suddenly find themselves in one of these fog pockets. This is when they hit the brakes, but by then it is often far too late.

During the day, the temperature rises and fog is changed back to water vapor. The fog is said to have "lifted." Freezing fog may stay too cold for the droplets to evaporate. Fog can last for several days until the moist air is replaced by drier, faster-moving air.

Photo Notes
- An aircraft sits fogbound at Hong Kong Airport.
- Moist air has cooled and condensed to form fog.
- The sun will heat the air and change the fog droplets back to water vapor.

Photo Notes

- A layer of photochemical smog lies over Los Angeles.
- Pollution from car exhausts and other chemicals is trapped over the city by mountains behind and warmer air above.

Pea Soup and Smog

A special kind of fog forms over many cities. This is called **smog**. It forms when chemicals from car exhausts and smoke from houses and factory chimneys get into the air and mix with fog.

Smog used to be a major problem in London. Smoke from burning coal mixed with car fumes and fog to give thick blankets of smog. It was said to be as thick as pea soup. In December 1952, the smog was so bad that about **3,500** people died from breathing problems. The elderly and people with bronchitis were most affected. After all these deaths, the government decided that it was time to clean up the air. Now there are smoke-free zones in most British cities where people are not allowed to burn coal in open fires. Cleaner forms of fuel have to be used instead. This has helped make the cities cleaner and the people more healthy.

Smog is a special problem in cities where air cannot rise or be blown away. This is what happens in Los Angeles. Exhaust from cars and buildings combine with sunlight to produce a dense **photochemical smog**. This can be seen as a thick, brown layer of pollution that hangs over the city. Cars have to pass tough anti-pollution controls, but the problem is still there. There are just too many cars.

In spite of new laws, smog still causes health problems to some people. Asthma is one health problem made worse by smog. This is why weather reports now give warnings of air quality when pollution levels become higher than normal.

DID YOU KNOW? **?**

In January 1993, all private cars were stopped from entering downtown Athens, Greece. The pollution level had become too dangerous for people's health.

The Deep Freeze

PEOPLE in some parts of the world are used to long periods of very cold weather. The lowest winter temperatures are in high mountain areas and inside the Arctic and Antarctic circles. Places with the greatest difference between hot and cold are in the center of the largest continents such as North America and Asia. When the cold weather comes every year, people who live in these places make sure they are prepared. Homes are insulated to keep in the heat and keep out the cold. Motorists learn how to drive on slippery roads, and equipment is ready to clear away snow.

Record Temperatures

It is hard to cope with a period of cold weather when the temperature drops to well below the average. Very low temperatures in winter bring snow instead of rain. A driving snowstorm is called a **blizzard**. Strong winds make the air feel even colder. This is called the **wind chill** factor.

In 1994, winter temperatures in the northeastern states were the lowest ever recorded in over 100 years. New York had its lowest temperature in 119 years. A band of land 1,250 miles wide, between New York and Minnesota was affected by the freezing conditions. People in these cities are used to winter temperatures that are on or just below freezing point at 32°F. The temperatures in 1994 were something very different.

In Dayton, Ohio, the temperature dropped to –26°F. It was worse in St. Cloud, Minnesota, at –40°F. By the end of January, the temperature in New York was down to –2°F. The average New York January temperature is just above 32°F.

Photo Notes
- Ice floating in New York Harbor in early February 1994.
- Scenes such as this are attractive to look at, but these conditions bring business to a halt.
- The very low temperatures were unusual, so people did not have the right plans or equipment to deal with the problems.

Winter Tales

The freezing temperatures brought chaos to the whole area. This is the part of the country where most people live and where a large amount of the country's industry and commerce is concentrated. People depend on power supplies and good transportation. The freezing temperatures disrupted power supplies, industry, and transportation.

Airports closed down, as they became unsafe. Snow and ice on the roads caused traffic accidents and some deaths. Tree branches snapped and brought down power lines. At the same time, the demand for electricity began to rise. Power stations had to reduce their voltage so that the system would not be overloaded. Factories and other businesses were asked to close down so that people could have heat in their homes. All 362,000 workers in the government offices in Washington, DC, were told not to come to work.

People who dared to walk about in these temperatures ran the risk of getting frostbite. Any part of the skin that is exposed can soon be affected. The death toll rose to 97 before the temperatures started to rise. Most of these were victims of traffic accidents. Others died from heart attacks when they tried to shovel snow away from their homes. A few died of exposure.

During the Big Freeze, there was a salt shortage. Supplies ran out, and sidewalks and roads along the whole eastern seaboard could not be salted. What salt was available was sold at very high prices.

This was not a winter that people will quickly forget. It was one that people were not prepared for, so they did not know what to do when it happened. It comes as a nasty reminder that no matter what people build or try to do, the weather sometimes has the last say.

DID YOU KNOW? [?]

The lowest recorded temperature in North America is –81°F, in Alaska in 1947.

Changing the Weather

Hᴵsᴛᴏʀʏ could have been different if the weather had been different. Battles on land and at sea might have been won by the side that lost. Some might not have been fought at all. Gales could have destroyed the invading fleet of William the Conqueror in 1066. It would be very useful to be able to control the weather. The U.S. Air Force tried to make it rain more heavily during the Vietnam War in the 1960s. The aim was to disrupt enemy supply routes, but it did not seem to work.

Rainmakers

It would be useful to be able to make it rain where there was a drought or to help put out a forest fire. Traditional tribal rainmakers try to do this by dancing and singing. Scientists use chemicals.

In 1946, an American scientist tried to make it rain by putting frozen carbon dioxide into the clouds. This is sometimes called **dry ice**. His idea was that since rain and snow form as ice crystals around tiny particles, the dry ice would help the process along. Putting something into a cloud is called **seeding**. The method seemed to be successful, so more attempts have been made to carry on with this idea. Clouds are now seeded using silver iodide and other chemicals. When it does rain, it is always hard to know whether the seeding has been successful or whether it would have rained anyway.

Large hailstones can flatten fields of crops. In the former U.S.S.R., rockets with silver iodide were fired into thunderclouds to try to make the hailstones smaller. They claimed that this reduced hail damage by **90 percent**.

Lightning can also be reduced by the same method or by dropping metal strips called **chaff** into a thundercloud. Electrical discharges on the metal strips help stop more powerful electrical charges from building up.

Photo Notes

- Large hailstones are made from ice crystals that have joined and grown to become large balls of ice.
- Hailstones can flatten crops.
- Scientists claim that they can make hailstones smaller so that they do less damage.

Changes by Accident

People do have some effects on the weather, though they are not always in ways that are intended.

Large urban areas are known to make their own "**heat islands.**" Heat escapes from buildings and vehicles and builds up in bricks and concrete. This can raise the air temperature over a city by a few degrees. The extra heat may be one reason why there are more tornadoes in the Great Plains than in the past.

Chemicals from cars, factories, and power stations rise into the air and come back down as **acid rain.** Sulfur dioxide is released when coal and oil are burned. In Norway, acid rain has been blamed for damaging up to 25 percent of the trees. Almost one-third of this is blown to Norway from coal-burning power stations in Great Britain. Fish and plants in lakes are also destroyed by acid rain.

Photo Notes
- Mining for tin in the Amazon rain forest in Brazil.
- Vast areas of rain forest are felled every year for mining, farming, and the timber industry.
- Changes to the natural vegetation and the color of the ground bring changes to the area's weather.

DID YOU KNOW? [?]

Scientists try to modify the growth of hurricanes by seeding the clouds. The aim is to make more clouds and more rain before they are sucked into a hurricane. This should reduce the hurricane's strength.

Changing the way land is used has an effect on the weather. The daily cycle of evaporation and rain in rain forests is broken when trees are cut down. Because of this **deforestation**, rain falls to the ground and flows away into streams and rivers, so there is less water to evaporate the next day. The land can soon turn into a dry wasteland.

A different land use causes the color of land to change. More heat is absorbed by dark surfaces than by light surfaces. Any change in temperature affects all aspects of the weather. It is very difficult to predict what or where these effects might be.

Greenhouse Earth

CLIMATES change. There was an Ice Age for about one million years that came to an end about 10,000 years ago. Winters in the Northern Hemisphere were colder between 1500 and 1900 than they are now. Cold weather we now call "extreme" may have been normal for the previous 400 years. One concern is that people are changing the earth's climates in ways that are hard to predict.

The Carbon Cycle

A real worry is the way in which the balance of gases in the atmosphere is changing. There is now about twice as much carbon dioxide (CO_2) in the air as there was 100 years ago. Carbon dioxide is a gas that is taken in by plants and changed to carbon.

The problem now is that carbon is being released at a much faster rate than before, mainly from burning coal and oil.

More **methane** gas comes from growing more rice and raising more cattle. Some scientists believe that these changes are creating a "**greenhouse effect**" that is causing a **global warming** of the average air temperature. This is bound to have effects on all aspects of the weather.

Photo Notes
- A world map shows how summer temperatures across the earth could change by the year 2050.
- Global warming caused by the greenhouse effect would change the earth's climates.
- The effects on the weather and on people's lives are hard to predict.

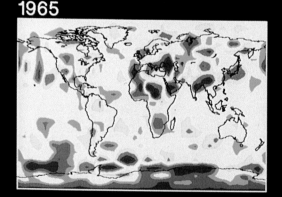

1965

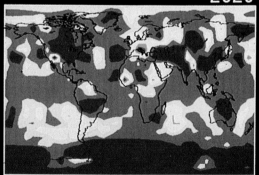

2020

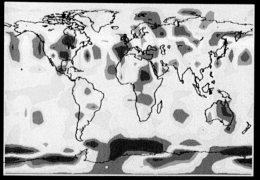

1990

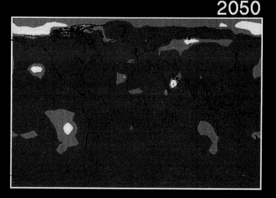

2050

The Greenhouse Effect

Heat from the sun comes through the atmosphere and reaches the ground as short-wave radiation. Some of this is reflected back to space as long-wave radiation. On the way back, long-wave radiation is trapped by some of the atmosphere's gases. Carbon dioxide is one of the main gases that does this. Heat is also trapped by methane and other gases. An increase in the amount of CO_2 and methane means that more heat is trapped. This is why these gases are called "greenhouse gases." They let the heat in, but they trap it on the way out.

The effects of an increase in the earth's temperature on the weather would vary from place to place. In some places, warmer weather could bring more thunderstorms, more hurricanes, and more tornadoes. Snow and ice would start to melt. This would change the color of the land so even more heat would be absorbed. World sea levels would rise as meltwater ran into the seas and warmer water expanded. The level could rise by several feet in the next 100 years. More storms and higher tides would bring a greater risk of coastal flooding.

Not everyone agrees that the greenhouse effect will give warmer climates for long. More heat would mean more evaporation and more rising air. This would produce more clouds, so less sunlight would get through the atmosphere. That could make temperatures lower. The problem is that all the different parts of the weather are linked in some way. One change has a domino effect on everything else.

Politicians from countries all over the world have tried to agree that by the year 2000, the amount of CO_2 in the air should be back to the 1990 amount. Not every country wants or can afford this. Some countries need more farmland and depend on selling timber to earn money. It would be very expensive to clean up the factories and the car exhaust. Warmer and more violent weather may mean it will cost even more in the future if nothing is done.

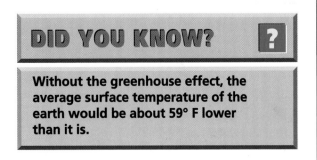

DID YOU KNOW? [?]

Without the greenhouse effect, the average surface temperature of the earth would be about 59° F lower than it is.

Glossary

acid rain rainwater with chemicals that are picked up from the air

air mass a large body of air that has its own temperature and moisture characteristics

air pressure the weight of air pressing down on the ground

anemometer an instrument to measure wind speed

anticyclone a weather system where there is high pressure

atmosphere the layer of gases that surrounds the earth

barograph an instrument that records air pressure on a revolving drum

barometer an instrument that gives a reading for air pressure

Beaufort scale a scale used to measure wind strength

blizzard snow that is being driven by strong winds as it falls

carbon cycle the way that carbon moves as a gas from the atmosphere to a solid form in plants and rocks, then changes back to a gas as they decay

carbon dioxide a gas given out when living things breathe and used by plants for growth

chaff metal strips that are dropped into clouds

cirrus a type of cloud at very high altitudes

climate the average weather conditions

cloudburst a sudden, very heavy downpour of rain

cold front a boundary line with warm air in front and cold air moving forward behind it

convection upward movement caused by heating at ground level

Corriolis force the effect of the earth's rotation on winds

cumulonimbus a type of rain cloud

cumulus large, fluffy cloud with rounded tops; often comes with sunny weather

cyclone *see* hurricane

deforestation the large scale removal of trees

drought a long period of time with no rain

dry ice a form of carbon dioxide that can be used to help make it rain

eye (of a hurricane) the central calm part of a hurricane

famine a time when there is a severe lack of food

flash (of lightning) a visible electric discharge

flash flood a sudden flood caused by a cloudburst

fog moist air that condenses at low level under calm conditions

forked lightning jagged lines of lightning

freezing fog fog in which the air temperature is at or below freezing point

front a boundary line between two air masses

gale winds that blow at speeds between 32 miles per hour and 63 miles per hour

global circulation the pattern of main winds across the earth

global warming a long-term increase in the temperature of the atmosphere

greenhouse effect the way in which some gases trap outgoing solar radiation

gust a sudden increase in wind speed

hail precipitation in the form of rounded drops of ice

hailstone an individual particle of ice that falls from the sky

heat island an area where there is a local increase in the air temperature

heatstroke a medical condition brought about by too much heat

hemisphere half of the earth

hurricane a weather system where there is an intense area of low pressure

hydroplaning gliding over a thin layer of water

isobar a line joining places with the same air pressure

jet stream a narrow band of very strong wind at high altitude

knot one nautical mile per hour, about 1.15 miles per hour

leader stroke the first link between negatively and positively charged particles in a lightning stroke

lightning a visible discharge of electrical energy from a cloud

lightning conductor a metal strip on a building used to bring a streak of lightning safely to the ground

low-pressure system a weather system where there is a center with low pressure

malignant melanoma a medical condition that is a form of cancer

mesosphere an upper layer in the atmosphere above the stratosphere

meteorologist scientist who studies the weather

methane a type of gas

monsoon a climate in which there is a seasonal change in the prevailing wind direction; sometimes refers to the rainy season

occluded front a front formed when two different fronts are joined

ozone a special form of oxygen

ozone hole an area in the ozone layer where there is a reduction in the amount of ozone gas

ozone layer a layer in the atmosphere where there is a thin band of ozone gas

photochemical smog a smog formed when chemicals in the air react with sunlight

precipitation all forms of water that fall to the ground, such as rain, snow, and hail

pressure *see* air pressure

pressure gradient the difference in air pressure between two places

prevailing wind the main direction from which the wind blows

radiation energy coming to earth from the sun

rain gauge an instrument used to collect and measure the amount of rainfall

return stroke the return of electricity along the path of a leader stroke when lightning is formed

savannah a type of climate in tropical areas

seasons groups of months that have a similar pattern of weather

seeding to drop chemicals into a cloud to try to make it rain

sheet lightning continuous flashes of lightning within a cloud

skin cancer a medical condition in which skin tissue is destroyed

smog fog mixed with smoke

snow a form of precipitation formed by ice crystals

soil erosion the process whereby soil is washed or blown away

storm a period of weather when winds are between gale force and hurricane force

stratosphere the layer in the atmosphere above the troposphere

stratus a type of cloud in layers

streaked lightning *see* forked lightning

stroke an electrical discharge between differently charged particles

sunshine hours the number of hours of sunshine in a day

sunstroke *see* heatstroke

temperature the level of heat, or hotness

thermal rising local current of warm air

thermometer an instrument used to measure temperature

thermosphere topmost layer in the atmosphere above the mesosphere

thunder the sound made by expanding air during a lightning flash

thunderstorm a rainstorm with thunder and lightning

tornado a narrow spiral of air rotating at very high speed

troposphere the lowest layer of the earth's atmosphere

twister *see* tornado

typhoon *see* hurricane

warm front a boundary line where warm air is moving toward an area of colder air

warm sector an area in a depression where warm air lies between a warm and a cold front

waterspout a narrow spiral of air rotating at high speed over water, sucking up the water as it moves

water vapor water in the form of a gas

weather forecast a prediction about the weather

weather vane an instrument used to measure the wind direction

willy-willy *see* hurricane

wind the movement of air

wind chill the effect that wind has in lowering the temperature

Index

Disasters mentioned in this book are printed in bold.